Farm Marketing From The Heart

Farm Marketing
from the Heart

How to attract your dream customers
to build your profitable farm.

Charlotte Smith

For my family, you are the reason I breathe:

Hayden, Austin, Shivan
and
Marc

Contents

Cover Photo by Alan Weiner Photography

Table of Contents

Click **here** for access to the bonus library for this book – This includes valuable resources and worksheets to help you learn what you can do to practice "Farm Marketing from the Heart."

http://www.3cowmarketing.com/book-resources-signup

Introduction

You probably picked up this book hoping for an answer to the question that you've felt overwhelmed with since the moment you started your farm: "How do I find more customers?" While that's a common enough question, it's actually the wrong question to ask when trying to market your farm products direct to consumer.

When you ask this question, you inevitably start scrambling to find ways to solve the problem of customers not being able to find you. Your marketing efforts center around getting rid of your product that's built up, whether it's a thousand chickens stored in a walk-in freezer all winter or veggies that will soon wilt in the summer heat.

You end up getting customers by any means necessary: discounting your products, delivering products all around town or even directly to people's homes, attending every farmers market in your area until you're frazzled. You're always searching for that elusive feeling of peace that comes from knowing every single item you produce will sell out at a sustainable price.

This desperation sets your farm up for failure because if you're always scrambling to find more customers, you'll end up finding the wrong customers. Now you may be thinking, "Wrong customers? Anybody with money in their pocket is the perfect customer for me!"

But there are indeed customers that can hurt your business. How do you know when you've got the wrong customers? They may be the ones that make you feel you need to justify why your prices are higher than the grocery store, or they don't show up when they say they will, or perhaps they always want extra favors or ask you to bend over backwards (when you're already overworked). They zap your energy and darken your mood, and soon you feel like you don't want to be around people at all!

Instead of asking, "How do I get more customers?" consider asking, "How can I find and serve my dream customers?"

Because when you have a whole slew of dream customers, you know how good it feels to send a single email and sell out of your whole season's worth of pastured chickens—so much better than worrying all year long, hoping to sell them before next spring's chicks arrive!

You know the joy of not losing half your customers after raising your raw milk prices by 30%.

And you have the peace of mind of knowing that you'll wake up to a voicemail inbox full of new customers clamoring for details about when you'll have more grass-fed beef available.

Those feelings are my reality, and by implementing the marketing mindsets and strategies I'll share in this book, you, too, will have similar experiences as you grow your farm business, raise your prices, and make a sustainable profit.

Farm-fresh food is in great demand, yet thousands of farms in America are going under each week. There is a way to stop that downward spiral and instead grow family farms that span generations while supporting the farmer with a decent living, and I'm on a mission to show farmers the way.

About five years ago, local farmers began asking me how I was able to sell out of all my products at the prices I needed to be sustainable and profitable, yet they couldn't sell out even when charging 30–50% less. I realized I needed to share my skills with other farmers, so I took what I'd learned over the years through education, training, and self-employment and founded 3 Cow Marketing, an online marketing training company for farmers. I've now helped hundreds of farmers embrace relationship-based email marketing and experience immediate results.

In Farm Marketing from the Heart you'll discover how to create a marketing plan to attract customers who loyally support your business. You'll learn how important it is to genuinely show you care for people and want to help them find solutions to their desires and struggles instead of just trying to sell your products. This willingness to go inside your own heart in order to better serve others is what I call "marketing from the heart," and when you put it into practice you will get in front of the right customers.

The right customers will love you and your farm so much that they'll tell their family and friends about you, helping your business grow by word of mouth. They'll drive an hour out of their way for product that costs much more than any neighboring farm, and they'll loyally return each season.

Going to farmers markets, making deliveries, or however else you sell your products is not a marketing plan. Marketing is not "build it and they will come." It's not "I hope I sell my product today." And it's not a one-off sale. Having a better vegetable CSA, charging less for raw milk, or growing flowers that are chemical free is not enough to get you the loyal customers you need to make your farm business last.

To make your farm business last, you need a proper marketing plan. A marketing plan is how you communicate the benefits of your products to the right customers, and it's a way to connect with people who will become loyal customers. When you practice marketing from the heart—which any farmer can learn to do—these customers feel like they matter to you. And when customers feel like they matter to the business, that they are important to you and you are looking out for their needs, they will shop with you again and again and refer their friends and community to you as well.

This book is going to give you the tools you need to begin to design an effective marketing strategy for your farm so you can stop the never-ending stress and scramble to find more customers.

There are two main components to farm marketing from the heart that you'll develop while reading this book. The first is the foundation upon which all of your marketing efforts will be built: your mindset. You may have a certain mindset that could potentially limit your growth and success as a business owner. You may believe things like, "I can't increase my prices to where I know they should be because the people in my area won't pay it." Or, "This won't work for me because I work a day job/don't have enough money/I'm introverted/fill in the blank."

But if you replace that limiting belief with the belief that you are here to serve your customers' needs, and you spend your days getting to know your customers, their desires, and their struggles, and you communicate how your products help them, you can and will be successful.

While I'm a big fan of strategies and tactics, none of the methods in this book will work without this strong foundation of the right mindset. Without the correct mindset, you'll find that the other strategies addressed in this book—having a productive website and a consistent email marketing plan—will just be generic tools that may advertise your farm but will not connect with your customers in a way that makes them want to buy from you. You won't necessarily stand out from any other farmer selling similar goods.

The second component of this book introduces you to powerful online marketing strategies that make it easier, faster, and more efficient to market and sell your products to your customers. In today's world, you need to have an online presence. Modern consumers want to research and connect with a business on the Internet before they make a purchase. They want to read reviews online, visit the company's website, check them out on social media, and chat with friends about the company's product.

One of the best ways to get in front of the right customers is to master a few basic online marketing essentials, including a simple website and consistent email communication, and then combine that with your copy—the words on your website that are written to attract the right customers. Then, when your dream customer reads through your website, she sees you have the solution to her struggles.

If you've been scared of technology until now, or thought you needed to spend thousands of dollars to get a website designed for your farm, don't worry. With our simple, free tech tutorials to get your online presence in place, you can even create a beautiful website yourself!

I know we're talking a lot about modern online marketing methods here, but the mindset behind marketing from the heart is ages old. It's really how people have been doing business for millennia. I first began to recognize the value of this mindset when I was waitressing during high school and college. Waitressing offers instant feedback. I found if I did a good job and was smiling and friendly and attentive, I got a larger tip. If I was distracted or rushed and not as attentive to customers, I received a lower tip. I made it a game: I would try to be as genuine and nice as possible, looking people in the eye and trying to anticipate their needs before they had to ask. Was the sun in their eyes and I needed to pull the shades? Or bring them extra napkins or plates for their children? I made sure they didn't have to ask for anything, and I'd make 25–50% more in tips than anyone else.

I realized that when I genuinely cared about the customers and I put my heart into serving people, I felt good about myself, I enjoyed the work, and I made more money. Not that I'm all about the money, but as a broke college student it made a big difference. I carried this mindset through my first few jobs, and when I started my own business I once again realized that just as important as the products I was selling was how much I cared for and even loved my customers.

At my raw milk dairy, it was easy to treat my first 25 customers like family. I would give them farm tours when they stopped in, share recipes with them, let the kids feed the calf its bottle. My customer base grew steadily with a constant stream of referrals. I was sold out on my first milk cow and had a growing wait list when I got my second milk cow. Soon, sold out with a wait list for milk on my second milk cow and all of our farm-fresh eggs, I got my third milk cow and more laying hens. By this point, around 50 customers a week were coming by my little store to pick up their milk and eggs, and we were so busy I was feeling a little frantic. I was not able to anticipate as many needs or give as many families the farm experience they were used to when coming out to shop with us.

About this time I noticed my customer growth had stagnated. Because I didn't have time to visit with all the customers regularly, some of the newer ones just didn't come back after a few visits. I was so busy it was a bit of a relief, yet it was also stressful—I knew I needed to keep growing our business by at least another 50% to reach a sustainable level of sales that would make all the cost and effort worth it.

I was searching all over for solutions to my dilemma when I began to notice online marketers using tools that I thought would streamline my marketing. After a bit of research and a couple training programs, I was able to create online systems that grew my customer base automatically, without having to spend precious time at farmers markets, making deliveries, or discounting my products just to make a few more sales. With this automated system in place to consistently and genuinely communicate and engage with my customer base, I found more and more people wanting to buy from my farm again. My time was freed up to engage with and serve them just like I had my first couple dozen customers, and I was able to maintain and even strengthen those relationships through my automated systems. Within a year I had reached my goal of serving 100 happy customers a week—the number I had figured would make me financially sustainable so I could stop worrying so much.

This book will help you achieve similar results, but it's important to read through the chapters in order because the concepts build upon each other. At the end of each chapter, I hope you will pause and take action on the material provided in the section "Your Next Step." Doing so will help you build the strong foundation you need to move on to each subsequent chapter and create your own plan to market from the heart.

Your vision for a farm that supports your family will become more of a reality as you read this book, focus on the right mindset, and learn to integrate a few tech tools with a genuine feeling of care for your customers. When you put the cares and struggles of your customers above the hustle to sell your products, just like I did, you will see the transformation in the bottom line of your farm.

1.

Chapter 1: Love Does Not Pay the Bills

Every week in America, 2,000 farmers go out of business. Just 80% make it to the two-year mark, and only 2% of farmers are in business after five years.

American author Wendell Berry has famously stated that given the economic adversities farmers face, we must do it for love, not for the money. He's right: Those of us who turn down lucrative job offers and cushy suburban homes to move out to the country and start farming don't do it for the money; we do it for love.

We love restoring the land. We love watching our children raise baby chicks instead of sitting in front of the TV all day. We love sitting down to a home-cooked meal fresh out of the garden. We love the feeling of sore muscles at the end of the day, knowing we put in a hard day's work instead of sitting in a cubicle for hours on end. We love the day-to-day surprises on the farm, instead of the mind-numbing monotony of a desk job.

But we soon learn love doesn't pay the bills. Love doesn't pay the electric company or your children's college tuition, and love certainly doesn't save your marriage after your husband finally says, "It's either the cows or me," a phrase I know many farmers have heard!

But does that mean to be successful business owners and farmers we have to ignore the part of ourselves that yearns for connection and love and instead turn into greedy, number-crunching salespeople?

Absolutely not.

In fact, the love that makes us such incredible farmers is also what makes us inherently skilled at marketing and selling our products. When you tap into your desire for connection and your natural inclination to care about people, and you then reflect that in the words you write and say to your customers, you set the foundation for a profitable, thriving farm so you can live your dream without the constant stress of wondering where your next paycheck is going to come from. Love doesn't pay the bills, but marketing from the heart makes it much easier to build a thriving farm business.

It's tempting to avoid the marketing side of running your farm, holding on to the belief that once you grow such an amazing product, customers will come flocking to you. However, you'll quickly realize that you need a reliable system to retain customers from year to year and to attract customers who won't balk at your higher-than-Walmart prices.

It's easy to believe that you'll be the exception to the rule and you'll make it past the two- or three- and even five-year mark running your farm. "I'm different," you say. "I have an MBA so this will be easier for me." Or maybe you have a degree in agriculture. Or a million dollars in the bank already. Whatever the case, if you go into farming with the mindset that you're the exception instead of the rule, you'll be out of business even faster! You must think of yourself as the rule—not that you'll be the 2% that's still farming after five years, but that you have an 80% chance of being out of business in two years!

When you think that way—when you're hungry and a little desperate—you'll be able to make the hard decisions that get you through to the next season and focus your efforts in the right place, instead of avoiding marketing altogether because it feels so overwhelming or uncomfortable.

It can be hard to find time for your marketing when you're dealing with all the moving parts on a farm. I know the struggle of milking cows, feeding the animals, collecting eggs, helping customers, and then still having to put together an engaging email to try to sell the quarters of beef at the butcher.

Despite everything else you have going on, you can learn to love marketing. You'll discover how fulfilling it is to connect with people in a meaningful way, adding value to their lives. You will build a customer base that respects your hard work and is happy to support your farm. Soon, you will find that the love of farming that was burning in you when you started can drive your desire to serve your customers and maybe even love them, too!

One of the best ways to start this process is to learn to build trust with your customers and potential customers. When customers trust you, they are loyal and will spread the word about your products and your service. I'll show you how to develop this trust in the next chapter.

YOUR NEXT STEP

Farmers struggle with marketing for many reasons, such as lack of time and marketing expertise, perhaps a feeling of being introverted. We also often feel like if we put our heart and soul and every last dollar into producing our products, then of course customers will find us!

Instead, I'd like to share a different perspective: If you have a product that is changing and improving people's lives (and yes, fresh veggies, flowers, soap, and other farm products do improve and change lives), then it is your obligation to get this product in front of your dream customers. It is not their job to find you.

As your next step for Chapter 1, I invite you to take a moment to visit the bonus resource library at farmmarketingfromtheheart.com and watch the short welcome video.

2.

Chapter 2: How to Build Trust with Customers When They've Never Met You

I often hear from farmers about how disappointed they are when they finally send out their spring newsletter to announce sign-ups for their CSA and less than half their customers from the previous year re-subscribe. Or perhaps they send out the form to order ¼ beef or ½ hog and don't have many repeat buyers, so they have to scramble to find new ones. Sound familiar?

Losing customers is frustrating, especially when you don't know why it's happening. But there's actually a very clear reason: you don't have a deep relationship of trust with your customers.

We all like to feel trust when we make even the smallest purchase. It's a feeling that is so obvious we aren't consciously aware of it. When we don't experience this feeling it's clear something is missing, yet we can't quite put words to it. "There was just something I didn't like about that person I bought the pigs from," you might say to your family. "I can't quite put my finger on it—the pigs are fine, but I won't purchase from them again."

To purchase anything, whether you're buying something online or running your credit card at the grocery store, you must in some way trust that business enough to give them your hard-earned money.

It's the same for your farm customers. When they trust you

to care about them and what they struggle with in life, and they trust that you care about how you can help make their life better, they are so excited to patronize your business. They tell all their friends about you. They're proud to showcase your products at their holiday meal or church potluck, and buying from you is one of the highlights of their week. And all this because you've let them feel how much you care about them and their lives.

Building trust with your customers is one of the foundations of marketing from the heart and of a profitable farm. But like any relationship, you must consistently nurture this feeling of trust. Without it, a person will shop from you once and move on because there's nothing bringing them back to you. You'll constantly churn through customers and spend all your time and energy trying to find new people to buy your products, wondering what you did wrong or blaming the world for your problems.

Building trust starts from the very first time someone hears about you, often before they've ever met you in person. A customer tells a friend about this amazing farmer down the road who sells the best eggs, and that person instantly trusts you because of this testimonial. Or maybe someone stumbles across your website and after reading a little about you, they're writing an email begging to be added to your wait list for raw milk.

If you're at a loss as to how to start building this unbreakable trust, one way is to start giving and sharing of yourself in ways that make your customer know she matters to you. Instead of developing your marketing plan based on convincing people to buy your product because it's better than the eggs you can get at Costco, you'll build a business based on giving.

When you come from a place of truly giving over and over, this naturally develops your customers' trust in you. I know what you're thinking: "I can't afford to give away my stuff; I have to charge for it!"

But I'm talking about giving away something other than your product—something that is free for you to give and something you know your customers are looking for. For example, giving of yourself and your expertise is entirely free. Give away your knowledge about the cooking or the increased nutrition of farm-fresh food. Give them a short tutorial on arranging fresh flowers. Invite people to your farm for an inspirational farm or garden tour, give a busy mom a 15-minute slow-cooker recipe that will get a healthy dinner on the table tonight, or share a video of you teaching your squeamish customers how to cut up a whole chicken easily. Even giving emotions such as empathy, compassion, and respect to everybody you meet will foster this deep relationship of trust.

When you build trust in this way, and especially as a farmer, you will be five steps ahead of other small business owners! Showing compassion and respect and sharing knowledge is easy to do in person, and when you learn to do it on your website and in your email marketing as well, people who land on your website or read your emails will get the same sense of trust and will want to buy from your farm instead of others.

When you have a marketing plan in place that's based on building trust and relationship with your customers and potential customers, you will sleep more soundly at night knowing that by getting your product into the hands of the people who need it most and who also trust you and willingly pay your price, you're helping so many people live their best life.

With marketing from the heart, you focus on one simple strategy: building relationships with people who need your product.

I receive emails daily from farmers wondering where the

best place is to advertise, or complaining that an ad they're paying for is not getting them any customers. I know it's tempting to think it's easier to just pay money for an ad instead of building relationships, but it's important to know that advertising no longer works like it did before the Internet—and many farmers have not realized this yet. Up until the mid-1990s, it was easy to buy a newspaper or TV or radio ad and reach a captive audience who would learn about your business and then shop with you. But in today's world there are too many options—people are on various social media platforms and reading any number of blogs and watching YouTube videos. When there are thousands of satellite TV channels, you couldn't possibly reach enough people with an ad. Simply put, there is no longer just one place that you could place an ad that would gain enough customers to support your farm. Yes, it requires some effort to build trust, but it works and it's necessary in today's world of very short and scattered attention spans.

When you spend the bulk of your marketing efforts giving to your customers, you'll stand out from all the other businesses that are competing for their dollars and constantly selling, selling, selling. They'll remember the email you sent them with a step-by-step video on arranging the perfect bouquet and delete the "On Sale, Buy NOW!" emails cluttering their inboxes. They'll tell their friends about the amazing workshop they took from you on how to make the best bone broth, and then they'll become a loyal customer for life. When your customers feel like they matter to you and that you genuinely care for them and want to help make their life better, there is absolutely no way that you're in competition with corporate big-box stores that make customers feel like they don't matter to them at all.

By now I hope you see why trust is so important. There are a few common roadblocks preventing farmers from building this strong foundation of trust, however. Some of these come along naturally with being a farmer and juggling all our responsibilities, and some of these roadblocks are personal. If you don't feel like genuinely trying to connect with your customers, then you won't be successful enough to stay in business. It might take some effort to find the willingness and desire to connect, but doing so is crucial to your success.

Here are a few of the struggles you may face as you embrace this mindset of giving and developing trust:

• I'm not a people person. How am I supposed to balance being an introvert with getting out and building relationships with people?

• I have so many customers that I can't keep up with all of them. How can I possibly give of myself to everybody without running myself ragged?

• I don't even like being around my customers. They suck up all my time and they're constantly complaining. What if I really don't want to spend time building a relationship with them?

First off, know that it's completely natural to have these thoughts and feelings. We're farmers, after all, and we likely got into this business because we like working with plants and animals better than being with people all day! But by honing your skills and practicing the strategies you'll learn in this book, you'll slowly start to realize that marketing isn't the drag you once thought it was. Instead, it'll become a natural part of your routine and leave you as satisfied at the end of the day as your sore muscles.

During my consulting sessions with farmers, it's not uncommon to meet people who just want to raise their chickens, cows, or veggies and not have to deal with people—they want someone else to do that side of the business. But that negative mindset is going to set the stage for your business and you won't have nearly the same success as the farmer down the road who understands some basics of human nature.

It's only natural for your customers to want to connect with you, their farmer. These people could buy from the corporate Whole Foods that's around the corner from their home, but they'll drive all the way out to your farm or fit the farmers market into their routine because they have an innate desire to connect with the person who's growing their food. If there's a bad connection, or if they don't feel a connection at all, they won't last long as a customer and you'll be scrambling to find more people to buy your product.

I'm as introverted as they come, but I know that to keep my customers coming back for more, I have to foster this relationship. Even if I've been dealing with customers all day and I don't feel like being chatty with someone who just wants to buy a dozen eggs, I have to dig down deep inside myself, call on my happiness reserves, and give some of that to the customer.

This may seem overly simplistic, but in a world of distraction, clutter, and busy-ness, people truly want to connect with you as their farmer instead of driving to the store to buy some organic veggies from a corporation. They want their kids to know the names of the cows that produced their delicious milk, and they want to look forward to seeing you every season to pick up their ¼ beef. They want to stop in and grab a flower bouquet and share a quick thought with you. While it's tempting to go to the farmers market or open up your farm stand and simply hope for sales, one-off purchases aren't going to build a successful business that makes it past the two-, three-, or five-year mark. Your customers make buying decisions based on connection, and by giving of your time and knowledge, you're taking the first steps to building a deep relationship that leads to repeat sales. But as with any relationship, it takes work to keep momentum going.

For instance, if someone comes to my farm store to buy five packages of T-bone steaks and 20 pounds of hamburger, I may think to myself, "Wow, that's awesome that I just sold all this steak and burger!" Sure, that will make a difference in my sales today. But I can't lose sight of the difference it makes to my business in the long term when I focus on the legacy of this interaction. So instead of assuming that the interaction with the customer is only about selling meat today, I can concentrate on sharing of myself, giving them my time, and fostering this deep relationship to ensure that they'll come back for more product.

Before I started producing raw milk, I bought several gallons a week from local farmers, and I distinctly remember the interactions I had with the farmers—or rather, the lack thereof. If I did happen to see the farmer walk by, I'd rush in, grab my milk, and race out before they got a chance to see me. I didn't want to run into them because they always seemed unpleasant, run ragged, and apparently not very happy to see me. Because my children needed the milk for health reasons, my weekly trip to get milk was a necessary chore, and I was stuck with the unhappy, tired farmer.

Unfortunately, none of them are in business anymore, which spurred the start of my own raw milk dairy. Now that I've been selling raw milk for several years, some of my customers have confided in me that they had similar experiences with other farmers. After a couple trips out to a neighboring farm, they never went back because the experience was so awful. But each and every week they look forward to making the trek out to my farm and chatting with my team or me, and they have been loyal for years. It's almost as if the raw milk is a pleasant bonus of our interaction!

So while sales are of course top of mind, what's more important with each transaction is to connect with our customer in some way, whether it's to compliment them on their outfit or their child, ask what they're using our product for, or share an interesting bit of information about the product they're buying. These seemingly small interactions help build trust, and people want to do business with companies and people they trust.

Now, say you don't interact with your customers on a regular basis—how are you supposed to build this relationship to keep your customers coming back for more? First, know that it's totally possible to maintain and even deepen your relationship with your customers even though you don't often interact with them in person. Of course, building relationships by visiting with someone in person is the best way! But as your farm grows, you'll eventually run out of time to see your customers in person often enough to make them feel like they matter, so you need to have other ways to connect. The rest of this chapter will explain how this works on my farm and how it helped me get some of my time back while still growing my business.

For the first several years of business, my farm store was self-serve. People pulled in to my driveway, got their meat and milk out of a little shed, and went on their way. Sometimes a customer would come and go for weeks without seeing me. If too much time passed, they lost that connection they initially felt with our farm and with me and eventually I began to lose customers. People would visit me two or three times, then I'd never hear from them again. The customer referrals and word-of-mouth marketing that I'd built my business on slowed down, and I felt like I was scrambling to get new customers and juggling to keep up with my current ones.

I found that I needed to touch base with someone about once per month and spend a few minutes connecting with them when they visited our farm, otherwise I'd eventually lose them as a customer. Fortunately, I stumbled upon a piece of technology that would change my business forever—an email marketing system. The email marketing system allowed me to build relationships with my current customers and reach new people without having to spend all day talking face-to-face. With one click, I could send out emails to my entire list of customers every couple weeks, and I was able to make them feel cared for just as if I'd been chatting with them at the farm.

These emails were very personal, as if I were writing to a friend instead of my entire group of 500-plus customers. I'd send them quick little recipes to help inspire them to cook the grass-fed beef I sold. Or I'd share some pictures of the baby calf born on the farm, or share a story of how one of my customers recovered from allergies and eczema after drinking raw milk. Then when I happened to chat with a customer in person, they'd tell me how much they loved the last email I sent them, or they'd thank me for the most recent recipe and share their experience making it.

This combination of in-person communication and email marketing has allowed me to scale my business steadily, have a wait list for many products, and grow to seven farm employees to help with the load.

I'm not the only one who's seen the difference marketing from the heart can make. After taking one of the free trainings I offer, Serena—who owns a diversified farm in Missouri selling pastured pork, beef, and chicken—experienced the power of email marketing combined with relationship building almost immediately. She set up her free email marketing system and started incorporating my suggestions on how to look for ways she could help her customers and offer solutions using her products. She began giving her customers helpful information she knew they wanted, such as meal planning and cooking tips, and the feedback was immediate! She had more clicks to her blog posts than ever before, customers felt like they mattered to Serena because of the way she was emailing them, and she received a record number of orders from her next email.

It's tempting to go to a farmers market and quietly stand behind your booth for a few hours or send a quick newsletter without thinking about who's reading it and think you've accomplished your quota of marketing for the week. But after taking our courses Serena realized that just being at a farmers market was not a marketing plan. She also realized that instead of standing in the market booth talking about her products and their health benefits, she needed to build trust with her customers. She needed to engage with them and learn about what's going on in their own lives and what's important to them. When she simply chatted with her market visitors about their day and engaged them in conversation, people walked away with purchases.

Serena didn't have to convince anybody to buy her meat; she didn't have to haggle over price or discount her products. She didn't have to spend hours studying buying psychology or marketing hacks, either. She simply sent her customers an email newsletter offering free information they had expressed to her that they wanted, and she connected with them in person. You can practice these same techniques and see results in your farm sales right away.

I know it's hard for farmers to juggle all our farm demands, care for our family and maybe even work a job off-farm, and still find time to build a customer base. But as Serena's story illustrates, it doesn't have to take a lot of time to build trust with people when you set up an effective email marketing plan and make just a little more effort to connect when you see them in person.

I will get into some more details of email marketing later in the book, but first we need to get a couple more pieces of our foundation in place.

In the next chapter, you'll discover how to focus your marketing to sell to the right customer so you can stop churning through customers from season to season and instead build a loyal lifelong customer base.

YOUR NEXT STEP

First, take the spotlight off you and put the focus on your customers when speaking with them face-to-face, whether you're at the farmers market, making deliveries, or hosting an event. The first words out of your mouth should not be, "My product is great because…" Instead, try these conversation starters to build trust and engage with a potential customer:

- "Have you ever tried grass-fed beef/raw milk/this product before?"
- "Do you have any fun plans for the weekend?"
- "Your purchases from that other booth look incredible! What are your plans for them?"
- Even a simple "I love your jacket!" (or earrings, kids, shirt—any compliment at all)

These questions might seem basic, but they're perfect to break the ice and engage with someone, putting the focus on them instead of trying to get them to buy.

3.

Chapter 3: What If All Your Customers Were Your Dream Customers?

Think back to your last transaction with a customer who purchased your product. Do you have one in mind? Maybe it was a phone conversation, an exchange at a farmers market, or someone who drove out to your farm.

After they handed over their money and you gave them the product that you worked so hard to produce, did you fall into the trap of thinking the transaction was over?

You may be thinking, "But they just bought my product, of course the transaction is over!"

Well, that kind of thinking is a huge mistake. Just focusing on individual sales is not going to make your farm successful, because those individual sales are not going to ensure you have money coming in weeks, months, and years down the road. Instead, they lead to a constant scramble to get new customers and convince new people to buy your product.

But if these individual sales aren't going to make your farm successful, what will? Loyal, repeat customers who love your product and are so proud that you are their farmer that they tell all their friends.

You know this is possible—heck, we've all had those crazy friends who camp out in front of the Apple Store the week leading up to a new iPhone release, or who stand outside a theater for hours waiting for a glimpse of their favorite band.

There are even hundreds of people who wait in anticipation every September for me to send out an email announcing it's time to reserve their Thanksgiving turkey before they sell out in 24 hours.

These loyal fan bases didn't happen by accident. It's a strategic move made by every successful business you know. Businesses like Apple, Amazon, and Whole Foods don't simply hope that people will buy their stuff. They know they're going to have consistent sales and loyal customers coming back for more. How did they do it? By getting laser specific on whom they are selling to. As business owners, we often forget that individuals, not the masses, buy from us. We get entranced by the idea of being as successful as Joel Salatin's Polyface Farm, and we tell ourselves we need to be famous like him to be profitable. But I'm here to tell you we don't need to be famous to have a successful farm.

In the desperation to be profitable, we forget who our customers are. We forget they're real people: parents desperate to heal their children, stay-at-home moms yearning for connection and community, young couples passionate about changing the corporate food system.

These individual people have feelings, desires, values, dreams, and fears. They're driven to seek out farm-fresh food for all sorts of reasons, and it is your responsibility as a business owner to understand what these reasons are. When you practice marketing from the heart, you learn to understand who your customers are, what makes them tick, and why they're buying from you. Some of these people are a great fit for your farm and make perfect customers. Others will drain your energy, exhaust your resources, and drag down your farm.

The consensus among farmers is often, "Everybody eats, therefore everybody could be a customer." If that way of thinking drives all your marketing efforts, you and your products become vague, general, and, honestly, boring. But by narrowing your focus so everything you do is to serve that one customer who has specific feelings, values, beliefs, and personal reasons for seeking out your farm, you are going to become irresistible.

The typical fancy marketing term for the one person you're selling to is your Ideal Customer; I like to call it your Dream Customer. It may sound intimidating, and it's easy to overthink the process, but walk through this exercise, and all your marketing efforts will fall into place. By knowing whom you're marketing to—in emails, on your website, on farmers market signs, in brochures, etc.—you can attract your dream customers to your farm and deter the ones who will not support your long-term business.

To identify your dream customer, first take a minute to imagine 2–3 customers you love. You wish all your customers were exactly like these people. You look forward to selling to them, and you appreciate all the business they send you by word of mouth. If you don't have customers yet, no biggie! Just imagine the dream customers you want to have in the future.

Do you have these people in mind? Okay, good.

Think about what it would be like to clone these favorite customers, so your entire customer base was exactly like them. That would make selling easy, right? I'm going to guess that they'd bring a smile to your face, they'd happily pay your price, and they wouldn't nitpick your farming principles. That person is your Dream Customer.

Now, you need to shift your mindset so instead of selling to everybody who has money in their pocket, you're only going to sell to that one specific person who is just like your favorite customers, and you're going to focus your entire marketing plan on this person.

What would you do to attract that one person? How would your marketing change if you knew you could forget about the masses and focus on just this one specific person?

When you write an email, you're going to write as if you are talking to that one dream customer face-to-face. You'll say things that your dream customer relates to instantly, like, "Hey Christie! Aren't you tired of trying to get a healthy meal on the table every day in between soccer practice and piano lessons? I know how it feels, which is why I'm so excited to offer you a brand-new weekly CSA delivery option."

When you create Facebook posts, you'll think to yourself, "Is this something my dream customer would love to share with her friends?" If that's a yes, you'll post it. If it's a no, you'll try something else.

When you design your website, you'll pick colors that your dream customer is attracted to. In your copy, you'll describe her unique struggles and make references to being a mom, or recovering from a chronic illness, or whatever stage of life she's in at the moment.

Then when a dream customer stumbles on your website or reads an email from you, she'll immediately feel connected to you because it's as if you read her mind. It's a no-brainer when a busy mom is looking for pastured eggs and she reads your brochure that says, "Our pastured eggs make the perfect breakfast so you can go from dropping your kids off at school to yoga class and not get hungry until lunch!" She'll pass over neighboring farms that sell pastured eggs for half the cost because she doesn't feel connected to them. Their marketing materials drone on and on about the farm's pasture rotation system, their locally milled GMO-free feed, and their latest soil analysis. A busy mom doesn't care about that; what she needs is a fast food for breakfast that's so full of nutrition that she won't get hungry as she's running all her errands. This is the power of marketing to one single person instead of playing it safe and generalizing your marketing message. And this is the power of marketing from the heart.

I often hear from farmers that "everyone" can buy flowers or vegetables, or everyone "should" be eating pastured meats. But I don't want to try to sell to everyone and have such a generic message that it dilutes my efforts. I don't want to invest time trying to sell to people who refuse to prioritize farm-fresh food in their budget; I want customers who put real food first. I don't want to justify the health benefits of raw milk to people all day long; I want a mile-long wait list of individuals who are begging me to sell them milk.

When I focus on only selling to people who fit my dream customer description, selling becomes fun and it's not even selling anymore—it's providing a service that people are grateful for. My customers are people I love talking to and who appreciate how hard I work to produce such high-quality food. They tell their friends about me, and my customer base grows with more people who fit my dream customer profile. These people would never dare buy raw milk or meat from just any farmer—they're loyal to me because I've built a relationship with them.

By focusing all of your marketing efforts on this one dream customer, you will attract more of your favorite people. You will be attractive to those people who fit your dream customer description, but not people who don't.

For example, my farm's website is pink and feminine in appearance. Even the front door of my farm store is pink because that's something my dream customer is attracted to (my dream customer is a woman aged 40–45). Perhaps some people are turned off by the design of my website and farm store, but since they don't fit my dream customer description, I will never try to persuade them to buy from me. (The funny thing is, even though my website is feminine and my farm store elegant, I have plenty of male customers who tell me how much they are drawn to my site and my store.)

My farm is located about 40 minutes from Portland, Oregon, a major foodie city. When someone begins searching for farm-fresh food in the area, whether it's grass-fed meat, raw milk, or a vegetable CSA, they're overwhelmed with hundreds of options. I'm right in the heart of the Willamette Valley, the grass capital of the world, and surrounded by farms of every variety, but I stand out from the hundreds of generic, boring farms in the area and have built a thriving, profitable farm because of my laser focus on attracting my dream customer and building a relationship of trust with her.

YOUR NEXT STEP

Who is your dream customer? Are you attracting your dream customer or are you inadvertently attracting lukewarm people who won't support your business and pay sustainable prices?

To get started, complete the dream customer exercise in the bonus resource library at farmmarketingfromtheheart.com.

Once you've created a description of your dream customer, put it into practice by creating a short post for your favorite social media platform. This could be a photo of a beautiful sunset on the farm, a quick meal-planning tip, a simple video of you creating a flower arrangement, or even a funny quote. As you write this post, ask yourself, "What does my dream customer need right now to help make her life better?" Pretend you're writing to your single dream customer and you'll notice how different it is from your previous generic posts!

4.

Chapter 4: You're Not Selling What You Think You're Selling

The benefit of updating your marketing materials to reflect your dream customer is that it will help the right people spot you in the crowd of local farms and grocery stores. But to start seeing results, you'll have to overcome another misconception most farmers have when they're just getting started. You may believe that you're selling eggs, or raw milk, or sustainably grown flowers, but thinking this way holds you back from reaching the hundreds of people who need your product. Why? Because you're not selling what you think you're selling.

Put yourself in your customer's shoes, or remember back to before you started farming. Trying to find healthy food or sustainably grown local products is overwhelming because there are so many options! In fact, the real-food and farm-fresh food markets are saturated with businesses all selling pretty similar products.

When people can get pasture-raised eggs at Whole Foods and most grocery stores, from the neighbor's backyard hens, or at the farm down the road, how do they decide? What makes people loyally shop from your booth at the farmers market each week for products that they can buy anywhere? Why would someone drive all the way out to your farm for U-Pick flowers when they can grab a bouquet for half the price at the grocery store? Today you can buy meat labeled "grass-fed" anywhere—heck, you can even order it online and have it delivered right to your door!

As farmers, you and I know the difference between these products, but busy moms trying to shop for their families don't know any different. To stand out in this saturated market and have people find you and buy from you, you must get super clear on what you're selling and then communicate this in your marketing materials. What do your customers experience after buying your product? What testimonials do you hear, or what has your own family experienced? What are the first questions you're asked when someone hears what you do? The answers to these questions will clue you in on what you're really selling.

For example, after my kids started drinking raw milk, their eczema disappeared. I'm not selling raw milk; I'm selling the solution that raw milk offers. I'm selling what moms have been searching for: a pharmaceutical-free cure for their kid's eczema.

As another example, several of my customers are moms who've adopted newborns and can't nurse them, and they are using our raw milk to make a healthy baby formula. So we're not selling raw milk; we're selling love and life for their newborn!

People don't wake up one day and out of the blue think to themselves, "I should start buying raw milk." Instead, they were looking for a solution to a problem they were having and came to the realization that raw milk (or fresh veggies, or pasture-raised beef, etc.) was the answer.

One of our marketing students, Lori, thought she was selling sustainably raised chemical-free flowers on her three-acre flower farm in Michigan. But after interacting with and truly listening to her dream customer, she found that they were coming to her for a moment of peace in their otherwise hectic day. They could stop in at Lori's roadside flower stand to pick their bouquet and while doing so enjoy reconnecting with nature and with other like-minded women. If these women were only looking for beautiful flowers, they would have gone to their local florist or even the grocery store. Instead, they drove out of their way to buy flowers from Lori.

When Lori finally identified that she was selling connection and peaceful moments and started sprinkling this throughout her marketing, she connected more deeply with her customers and found it even easier to sell her flowers. Selling and marketing were finally fun for her!

If she told people to buy her sustainably raised chemical-free flowers, it fell on deaf ears. Instead, she "sells" the peace and serenity women feel when they visit her beautiful garden. She sells a moment of quiet in an otherwise very busy day. And her customers connect with this and love to shop with her.

You might have experienced this struggle without even realizing it. Have you ever had a conversation with a potential customer and felt frustrated that they didn't seem to care about how much better your products were than store-bought? Maybe you felt angry after watching people's eyes glaze over while you talked about your sustainable farming methods, and you wondered why you don't have very many repeat customers.

Or you explained your raw-milk safety precautions in detail, listing the chemicals you use and the special mineral blend your cows receive, and simply got an "Oh, that's interesting" in response. Or maybe you write an email to your customers explaining the ingredients of your homemade bug spray and the compost strategies you use, then wonder why nobody buys your veggies.

The truth is, your customers don't care. While it's fun to chat with our farmer friends about the grass seed blend we got at the local ag store, our customers aren't farmers, and they couldn't care less. Whether in person, on our website, or in emails, when we only talk about the attributes of our products or the details of our farming practices, and we don't invest time to find out what our customers' needs really are, they subconsciously feel that we don't care about them and their interests. They lose trust in us, the relationship peters out, and they stop buying from us.

If you love to talk about your farming methods, then get together with other farmers and talk about them! But when you're marketing your farm and your products, you cannot assume that consumers want to hear all the nitty-gritty details.

Again, you're not selling what you think you're selling.

Your customers are looking for healthy, real food. They're busy and want to get dinner on the table with as little fuss as possible. They want to connect with their farmer instead of shopping from a corporation.

Step into your dream customer's shoes for a moment. Imagine you're looking for grass-fed beef, so you do a Google search for grass-fed beef in your town.

Several websites pop up, and you check them out. They say things like, "Beef—100% grass-fed and grass-finished. Versatile Dexter breed. Call to purchase." Or "We raise our cattle on pasture that's fortified with minerals that most soil is lacking. The cows are rotated to fresh grass every 24 hours, and they are never fed any grain."

Unless you're a farmer and you know this lingo, your eyes have glazed over, and you're ready to click to Facebook for something more entertaining. But then you stumble on my farm's website and read through everything, finally landing on my Products page where I describe what I sell:

If you've landed on our website you're most likely looking to improve your health through food. We can help. Take a look around and whether it's bone broth for digestive discomfort or raw milk for allergy relief, you'll find something that will help.

Ground Beef: Easily the most versatile product we provide—you should always have plenty to spare for those nights you feel totally and entirely uninspired and have no intention of getting there. Grill it, loaf it, fry it up with some kale and sweet potatoes for the ultimate paleo dinner without much effort.

Pastured Chicken: The ultimate in buying bulk, one of our chickens will feed your family for two nights with the effort of only one. Roast chicken the first night, lettuce wraps, enchiladas, or soup after that. You'll have enough time on the "leftovers" day to schedule that pedicure your toes are desperate for. And the family still eats!

As you can see, I'm not selling ground beef and pastured chicken.

I'm selling the solution my product offers: quick, easy, healthy, paleo-friendly meals that any busy mom can make. Using actual words I've heard from my dream customer such as, "I'm totally uninspired when it comes to making dinner night after night," I show her that I understand her. And when I give her a few suggestions to make dinner easier, she's so grateful.

How do I know what my product does for people? There's no special trick to it—I just ask them! When a customer is buying something from you, it's the perfect opportunity to engage them in conversation and learn about their challenges and how your product helps solve them, but most times the farmer or employee just completes the sale and moves on or goes back to looking at their phone. I witness this all the time at farmers market booths.

Let me show you how I do it instead. When a customer comes into my store and picks out a roast, I'll ask how she plans on cooking it or if it's a finer cut of meat I'll ask if it's for a special occasion. I want to make conversation and show interest in her. Remember, this helps her trust me even more. I'll also ask if she's seen our recipe booklets, which are free for the taking, and I might show her one or two options for recipes she can try with the particular cut of meat she purchased. Without much cost or effort on my part, I can give her a valuable gift—a recipe that saves her some time and gives her fresh inspiration, something my dream customer is often looking for when it comes to cooking dinner.

She's so grateful for the conversation and that I engaged with her and then gave her more ideas. And many times, once I start talking with my dream customer about how she's going to cook a particular cut of meat, she ends up going back for more cuts because our conversation inspired her to try a new recipe!

Because I'm not always in the store, I keep a notebook there that includes reminders for employees on what to say to customers and has space where they can make notes after a customer interaction, such as what recipe the customer was buying the product for and what questions they asked. This information allows me to stay on top of customer service and respond to specific customer inquiries (for example, "Betsy wants to know if she can have her chickens cut up this year instead of whole"), and gives me tons of insight into my dream customer's likes and dislikes as well as material for future emails and blog posts (based on Betsy's question, I might determine I need to be more specific in my email about ordering chickens).

So when I ask you what you sell, I don't want to hear that you sell grass-fed beef. I can run down the street to my local grocery store and find grass-fed beef, so there's no reason to buy from you. But if you sell a way to get a super-healthy dinner on the table fast or a way to feed their adopted baby a healthy formula when they can't nurse, you are selling so much more than the products you raise.

When you embrace the mindset that you aren't selling flowers or beef or eggs, but instead you are selling a solution your dream customer is desperate for, you will find that the potential customers who read your website will be excited to come out and purchase from you! They feel like you "get" them. They feel so deeply connected to you that they can't wait to call you "their" farmer and support you. Soon they are telling their friends that they must shop with you. When you practice marketing from the heart in this way, listening and offering solutions to your dream customer's struggles, sales grow and your farm thrives.

YOUR NEXT STEP

First, I have a worksheet in the bonus resource library over at farmmarketingfromtheheart.com that will help you discover what you're really selling—it walks you through how to find out this information from your dream customer.

Then, pick one of your marketing materials to update with the new information you've uncovered. Your marketing materials might include your website, blog posts, email communication, social media posts, signage for farmers markets, brochures, etc.; for this exercise, you might want to start with the one that's easiest to edit.

Instead of listing your products and describing your superior sustainable farming practices or your unique process, appeal to the problems your dream customer solves by using your product. Try adding a sentence such as, "If you're a busy mom wanting to get a healthy meal in your family at least once a day, then you're in the right place! Our meat products are the perfect solution!" Or maybe, "Looking for a bit of peace in an otherwise busy, cluttered world? Join us in our tranquil urban garden for a Farm Tour this Saturday."

5.

Chapter 5: Charge Sustainable Prices (No Matter What the Neighbors Are Charging)

As if farming and marketing aren't hard enough, when it finally comes to selling our products that we've put thousands of hours (and dollars) into, we often have to listen to people complain about the prices. (If I had a dollar for every time I heard, "You charge what for a dozen eggs? I'm going to Costco," I'd be a millionaire!)

Of course, you and I know that our farm-fresh products don't even compare to store-bought, yet we face a society that treats food as a commodity. When people believe the cheaper, the better, quality notwithstanding, it makes selling our product feel like a chore.

Customers try and guilt us into charging low prices, and it's easy to feel like we are in competition with grocery stores. This is one of the biggest mistakes farmers make as they're just getting started, because we can never compete with grocery store food prices. Industrial organics rule the supermarkets and even some farmers markets. Food prices are kept artificially low with government subsidies and propped up with slave labor. By trying to compete on price, you are doing a disservice to you, your family, your customers, and our food system.

The alternative is to take ownership of your prices and confidently charge what you need to make a sustainable profit. I completely understand that this is an intimidating concept, but when you practice marketing from the heart and start to build deep relationships of trust with your customers, you will actually have their complete support in charging sustainable prices.

I often receive emails from farmers who've decided to raise prices and are either sending me feedback or are asking for help. Recently, two different raw milk farmers shared with me their story of raising their prices after realizing their costs far outweighed their income. I thought it was very telling that these stories came to me around the same time but had two very different outcomes.

The first farmer shared in a frantic Facebook post that she was desperate for help because she lost 60% of her customers after sending an email announcing she was increasing her milk price by 40%. The other farmer who contacted me, Carla, had raised her raw milk prices by 60% and had a completely different outcome. Carla is one of our students, and she had recently started mindfully practicing marketing from the heart. When she then sent out her price increase notice for her raw milk, she did not lose one single customer because of the relationship of trust she'd built with them.

I receive stories similar to both of these at least once a month—either a "thank you for all the relationship-building strategies, it went great!" or "I heard you might be able to help me. I lost half my customers when I increased my prices. What did I do wrong?"

I see farmers pouring their savings into their farm to subsidize their products, or working a day job in the city to support the family. They feel helpless to increase their prices, as if external forces are determining what they can charge. When you say things like, "I can't charge that much for my product," you are giving away control of your success. If you don't think you have control over your pricing and instead hold the belief that the market determines what you can charge, then you'll most likely be out of business in a few years.

The more often you tell yourself these things, the more opportunities you'll miss that would have allowed you to build a sustainable farm and business. Instead of looking for a solution, you get stuck in a "victim" mindset that prevents you from expanding your business and seeing new areas for growth.

It can be tough to recognize that it's our thoughts that are holding us back. But it's actually a good thing, because how our mind sees things and the way we think are completely up to us! We can change our mind in an instant and see results immediately.

The truth is, your lack of customers is completely under your control. It's not the neighbor's low prices or the lack of foodies in your community that are stopping your farm's growth. It's your thoughts that are stopping your business from being successful. Your farm can be successful no matter where you live and who surrounds you, even when you have no time between running the farm and your day job, or you're an introvert, or you don't have enough money.

Limiting beliefs, such as thinking that outside forces determine your prices or that you can't change the fact that no one is beating your door down to pay you a fair price, limit your chances of success. As soon as you think to yourself, "This won't work for me because [fill in the blank]," you might as well call it quits, because you'll never give yourself the chance to try something new that will help you be successful.

By now you may be thinking, "Why is Charlotte writing about thoughts and mindset yet again?" It's because every time I write a post for farmers on marketing your farm and include some marketing tactics that I know work well, I get some comments from people saying they tried them and they are working; their farm is growing and doing great and finally making enough to pay the bills. But I also get comments from some who say, "This sounds good but won't work for me because…" and share any reason (or excuse) that implementing these new ideas and techniques won't work for them.

Next time you catch yourself thinking, "This won't work for me because…" instead think, "I can make this work if I just try this…" With that one simple shift in your thinking, you'll unlock your potential to innovate and grow.

Yes, there will always be cheaper farms surrounding you. Every industry has their trust-fund babies who start a business and for whom profit isn't an issue, or the businesses that cut corners to produce cheaper products than you.

When it comes to farming, low prices are often how farms compete. Unfortunately, competing on price isn't a marketing plan, so when farmers realize they need to raise their prices, they lose all their customers.

Marketing from the heart—by identifying your dream customers, building a relationship of trust with them, and showing them that you have the solutions they are looking for—will bring you customers who will encourage you to charge a sustainable price. It won't matter to them what anyone else in the area is charging because they trust you as their farmer and they want you to remain in business for years to come!

The practices for marketing from the heart that you've learned so far, combined with the confidence to charge the prices you need to be sustainable, will help get you set up for our next chapter, where we focus on a system to help make your marketing efforts more efficient.

YOUR NEXT STEP

Now that you've gone through the exercise of identifying your dream customer, it's easier to let go of people who aren't a good fit—which includes customers who complain about your prices.

Instead of apologizing or explaining the true costs involved in producing your products, an easy way to move on from the uncomfortable situation where someone complains about your price is to simply tell them, "I understand that our products are not for everyone." I have many farmers email me saying how that phrase frees them up. They no longer feel obligated to justify their prices; instead, when people complain about price it helps them realize that person is not a good fit or not their dream customer.

Once you make the mindset shift that it is your obligation to charge sustainable prices so you're in business years down the road, it will become easier to focus your attention on your loyal customers and do everything you can to serve them best.

If you've avoided charging what you should because you've been afraid of losing customers, then head to our bonus resource library at farmmarketingfromtheheart.com; the How to Increase Your Prices without Losing Customers worksheet will help you build a plan to do just that.

6.

Chapter 6: The System for Consistently Attracting New Loyal Customers

Now that you've developed a strong foundation—you know who your dream customer is and how you can serve her and give to her to build trust—you're ready to develop your online presence with your website and email marketing. This is the system that will allow you to consistently attract new loyal customers and build a profitable, sustainable farm.

While it's tempting to want to skip ahead to the strategies and tactics you'll learn in this chapter, you'll be marketing to deaf ears if you haven't solidified your mindset and built your strong foundation, so be sure to read and implement the chapters in order.

For example, before creating a website, you must know your dream customer, otherwise you'll be guessing as to what words, phrases, colors, photos, or product descriptions to use to connect with her so she reads it and wants to do business with you. If you don't design your website with your dream customer in mind, she will land on your site, not feel a connection to you or your products, and immediately click away. Before writing emails to her, you also must know what kinds of questions she has, what topics are interesting to her, and what she's struggling with in life.

When your website is attractive to your dream customer, she will land on it after being sent by a friend or perhaps searching for your product, and she will think it's just for her! She will see herself in the phrases you've written on your website (a result of the work you did in Chapter 4, where you discovered the "solutions" you're selling rather than your products). She will connect with your solutions to her struggles and desires, and she'll want to sign up to receive your emails to learn more.

With all the recent advances in technology, it's so much cheaper and easier to put up a sophisticated website yourself without spending thousands of dollars like I did when I started my farm years ago. As a result, customers expect sophisticated and attractive websites—but I'm here to tell you it's not difficult to do yourself; many of our students get an attractive and effective website in place in just one day.

Then, to save time and make your communication far more effective, you've got to have an email marketing system in place (don't worry, there are great free options out there). Not only is it more efficient, an email marketing system is the only legal way to send mass emails to your customers (yes, using the blind copy feature in your regular email account is breaking the anti-spam laws!).

The power of online marketing is responsible for the success of many small businesses, yet this technology hasn't reached most farmers yet. While I'm selling out of my premium-priced raw milk and pastured meats, neighboring farms that sell the same product for half the cost are struggling to make ends meet because they haven't taken the time to create the systems that build a loyal customer base. However, when you practice marketing from the heart and you combine consistent relationship building with an effective website and email marketing technology, you create a powerful and productive marketing system for your farm.

Let me walk you through how this system turns a potential customer into a customer and then repeats the process, consistently building your customer base.

Imagine someone is searching for grass-fed beef because they just joined a CrossFit Box and this new community is encouraging them to eat paleo, including pastured meats. Lots of generic farm websites come up in her search that all have similar info and list a short product description and the price. Then she clicks on my website. She immediately feels a connection of trust with me and feels like I "get" her. She signs up for my free gift, "5 Tips For Cooking Grass-Fed Beef Perfectly Every Time," which also subscribes her to my email list. Now she trusts me even more because before she's ever purchased anything from me I'm giving her free, helpful advice to make her life better or easier.

She starts receiving my emails, which feel like personal notes addressed to her about my farm and how I can serve her. At the bottom of my email, after I've engaged with her about what I know my dream customer wants to hear from me, I share clear information on how to buy our grass-fed beef, and she becomes a customer for life who will support me any way I need to make sure I stay in business!

This is how I built my profitable and sustainable farm: a productive, effective, and pretty website directed towards my dream customer; an email marketing system to connect with them and build trust; and consistent interaction with my dream customers. Every single person who walks into my farm store and becomes a loyal customer has at some point met me in our community, stumbled across my website, or connected with me via email or reading blog posts and immediately sensed that I had the solutions they were looking for. They felt such a strong connection and sense of loyalty that they now spend hundreds or thousands of dollars a month on my products, assuring my farm remains sustainable.

You'll notice I didn't mention anything about paying for ad space in the local newspaper. I didn't spend hours obsessing over my farm's Likes on Facebook, and I didn't run specials or discounts.

You can replicate this system for your own farm, just like the hundreds of farmers I've helped personalize their own plan to attract new email subscribers; nurture their relationship with them by giving them free information, education, or inspiration to make their life better; and then earn the right to sell to them.

In our final chapter, I'll talk about what you can do now to transform your farm by marketing from the heart.

YOUR NEXT STEP

If you haven't already, now is the time to explore the modern (and affordable) technologies I recommend you use to take your marketing online: your website and your email marketing system.

In the bonus resource library at farmmarketingfromtheheart.com, you'll find more than 15 technology how-to videos that walk you through the process of creating your very own low-cost website using Squarespace and integrating it with MailerLite, a free email marketing system. These videos are specific to farmers and will get you up and running with your own online presence.

Even if you already have a website, the videos are worth a watch; they will give you all sorts of ideas that are specific to making farm websites more effective.

7.

Chapter 7: Put It All Together to Live the Farm Life You've Dreamed Of

The struggle for farmers is real, and it's part of our daily routine. Cows die. Aphids invade the flowers just before harvest. The lettuce bolts in a couple unseasonably hot days. The milk tastes "off" one week and everyone complains. Or you wake up at 2:00 AM worried about finances. Again.

I communicate with hundreds of farmers each week and we encourage each other in our inevitable farm struggles. My dream is that with this small book I can help ease the struggle of marketing your products so that it becomes an enjoyable process for you instead of something you dread.

Now you're aware of the mindset, skills, and tools needed to build a heart-centered marketing plan for your farm. You understand the importance of establishing a foundation with a mindset of serving and giving to your customers; you've learned a process to identify who your dream customer is and what desires and struggles you help her with. You know the importance of having a simple website along with an email marketing system, and you've begun building a relationship with your dream customers.

At this point, most of my students have one of two questions: "How do I get more customers on my email list, besides my mom and three friends?" Or, "What if I have all the wrong customers and I need more customers who will support my prices?"

Remember, in the first couple pages of this book I said that these are the wrong kinds of questions to be asking. When you focus on finding new customers or getting people to find your farm, you inadvertently shift your focus from serving people to finding more customers by any means necessary. This may include coupons or discounts, advertising your products, talking about your farming practices, and trying to be louder and bigger than the competition so customers will choose you over someone else.

If you've done this in the past and you now have the wrong customers—ones who force you to justify your prices, don't stick around, and leave you constantly looking for new customers—you can definitely start transforming these current people into loyal customers at the same time you begin to add new loyal customers to your base.

Instead of asking how to find more customers, ask yourself how you can serve one customer today. That gets you thinking of ways to give. When you show up at your farmers market booth for the day from a place of service, your dream customer will feel like she matters to you, which opens the door to her buying from you. And when you ask her to sign up on your email list right there on the spot—on your phone or iPad or even a low-tech email sign-up sheet—so you can continue to communicate with her, she'll be delighted to.

If you had just shown up at the market with the mindset of trying to sell as much product as possible and hurry back to the farm, you'd miss out on building a relationship with potential long-lasting loyal customers. Because when these customers meet you in person and instead of focusing on selling to them you give of yourself, they trust you and feel connected to you and want to hear more from you.

When you invest time in showing up at the market or your store or in your community and listening and engaging with others, sharing your skills or your knowledge, you'll connect with people in a much deeper way than with online marketing alone. By listening to people's struggles and desires, you'll learn tidbits of information on who your dream customer is inside and out so you're always fine-tuning how you can communicate the solutions you offer through your products.

One of our students, Sarah, does this beautifully. Sarah owns a flower farm in Iowa where she sells cut flowers and offers a variety of wholesale and retail options including bouquet subscriptions, wedding and event florals, and flowers at farmers markets. Her dream customer is a young, busy mom who enjoys gardening with her kids and sprucing up her house with fresh flowers.

Since Sarah's local library already attracts plenty of moms who are looking for activities to do with their children, she hosts free gardening workshops there. The library is happy to get the word out to their community, a large group of women Sarah otherwise never would have met. While she's teaching the workshop, she's building relationships with these women who are excited to join her email list right there on the spot because she has freely shared her expertise and taught them a valuable skill. This is all done very casually—they can just pull out their phones and sign up on the website (like you learned to set up in Your Next Step from Chapter 6)—and this gives Sarah the opportunity to continue strengthening a relationship with them through email after the initial in-person connection. Plus, the students tell their friends about the wonderful woman who sells gorgeous bouquets and gives the fun, free workshops at the library.

Sarah wasn't giving the workshop to sell; she was teaching it to give to her dream customers. And in doing so, she's building a thriving business. That is the power of farm marketing from the heart.

Many of my hundreds of raw milk customers came from the time I spent in the first few years of business offering free demos of yogurt and kefir making. I would invite someone into my kitchen to watch me make yogurt or kefir, or I would do a demo at a local event to show people the process. I earned credibility and built trust through this simple act of showing them something I do every day that seems so foreign to them but they want to learn how to do. They couldn't wait to come out to the farm and make their own purchases, and we continue to keep in touch via my twice-monthly emails where I share even more things they want to hear about.

How could you use your community to reach more of your dream customers like Sarah did by offering workshops at the library or I did by offering cooking demos? Consider the places your dream customers are already going: CrossFit boxes, health food stores, community centers, mom's groups, book clubs, cooking classes, Kiwanis and Rotary Clubs, yoga studios, gardening clubs, homesteading supply stores, and more. These businesses and organizations are usually eager to offer something new and different, so they will be grateful to host your event or demo and share your event information with their connections.

It's important you keep in mind that these are great marketing opportunities but not necessarily profitable secondary income streams. You can certainly charge for your workshops, but the bigger benefit to you is that you build trust with all these people by giving to them. Those that feel a connection with you will want to get on your email list, where you can continue building a relationship of trust with them so they eventually become customers.

Within your heart-centered marketing plan, it's important to find ways to connect with people with the intention of giving and serving, not selling your products. Be prepared to show up and teach your class for free and have no one buy a thing. But trust that your returns will be so much more immense: You will become known as a trustworthy source of helpful information and become a household name in your community. People will refer their friends to you and your business will start to grow steadily with the right kind of customers—your dream customers.

Most farmers are unsure where to focus their community outreach or where to start marketing, but now that you've identified your dream customer you can spend your time in the right places! Perhaps you can team up with a community member to make your products more accessible. For example, let's say your dream customer is a fitness enthusiast like Melissa's.

Melissa owns a flower-and-herb CSA in Maine and helps another friend market their pastured-meat products. She also does CrossFit five days a week (and has biceps to die for because of it!). She approached the owner of the CrossFit Box and suggested he have a meat freezer at the gym so she could deliver meat orders—this way, CrossFit and paleo diet enthusiasts could get their workout in and their grass-fed beef at the same time, which would make this particular box stand out in their community and attract more members. Melissa found an instant community of 200 people interested in her product, and the gym owner found one more way to serve his customers, too. Perhaps there are places in your community you can reach out to, just like Sarah and Melissa did, and tap into a group of people you can introduce your product to.

Marketing is not about being cheaper than your neighboring farm, nor is it about jumping in to interrupt people's day at the farmers market. It's not about convincing people to buy your products. Instead, when you practice marketing from the heart, you connect deeply with people and give them solutions to something that's holding them back or offer them something they've dreamed of. Marketing from the heart is about showing people we care about their lives, their dreams, and their struggles, and we've spent time figuring out how we can help them.

When you have your heart-centered marketing plan in place, you'll find you soon have a loyal group of customers who support you in charging the prices necessary to keep you in business for the long term. Finally, you will be part of that 2% that makes it to the five-year mark of running a profitable farm and even far beyond, perhaps having a sustainable farm to pass on to your children.

The personal connections you form in your community, along with your strategic website and consistent email communication, will help ease your marketing struggles. Remember, one doesn't work without the other—you can have the fanciest website and the most intricate email marketing system, but without the trust and loyalty of your customers, you won't make sales.When you operate a small farm, whether you produce flowers, vegetables, meat, eggs, dairy, or artisan goods, you're offering products that are changing people's lives in tremendous ways. It's up to you to get them in front of the people that need them most.

I've written this book to help ease your marketing struggles and certainly not to overwhelm you! Marketing from the heart will transform your farm—I hear and see this with hundreds of farmers every single day. If you're inspired and want to join us, I hope you'll take it one chapter, one step at a time and see how good it feels to be confident in serving your dream customers. Then watch your farm flourish and grow so you can finally live the farm life you've dreamed of. This is the power of farm marketing from the heart.

YOUR NEXT STEP

In the bonus resource library at farmmarketingfromtheheart.com, the Community Resource List offers ideas of places and people you can tap into to reach more of your dream customers.

Don't let all the possibilities overwhelm you—instead, use this list to inspire you to think of people or businesses that might already attract your dream customer, then make a point to reach out to one of these each week.

Schedule one day/time each week that you can commit to building more connections in your community. For me, that's every Wednesday afternoon. I have a couple hours set aside after lunch and before school lets out when I can make a phone call to chat with a potential connection, email a few prospects, or even drive out to meet with a business I've connected with recently and share with them my ideas of spreading the word about my products with their connections.

About the Author

Charlotte Smith owns Champoeg Creamery & Pastured Meats, a 75-acre diversified farm selling raw milk, pork, chicken, and beef direct to consumer. She founded 3 Cow Marketing, an online marketing training company, when she realized the struggle farmers face when trying to build a farm business that supports them instead of breaks them. Charlotte lives and farms in St. Paul, Oregon, with her husband, Marc Rott, and is the proud mother of a United States Marine, Austin, and two astounding daughters, Hayden and Shivan.

Acknowledgements

Although the ideas, thoughts, and stories are my own, it would not be the book it is if not for my daughter, Hayden, who poured over every word – too many times to count. If I struggled with finding just the right phrasing or a better example, or if a certain chapter didn't seem to flow right, she always knew the perfect solution.

Hayden, I am so grateful for your knowledge, courage and your wisdom, but greatest of all, you are my beautiful treasure of a daughter, and it's been a mother's dream to be able to work by your side through this project! Thank you.

Huge thanks to my editor, Amy Scott, of Nomad Editorial. Your suggestions, expertise and writing finesse improved my work ten-fold! And the icing on the cake was that I got to meet you in person while you were traveling across the country and landed on our farm for an afternoon.

I would not be the woman I am if not for my partner and husband, Marc Rott – every single day you tell me how much you love me and how amazing I am. You devoted countless hours, many of them in the wee morning hours or late evening hours, to keep the farm running smoothly so I could take the time to write. I am eternally grateful for you and your continuous love and support.

Lastly, to the 144 farmers in my book launch group – I am deeply indebted to you. You milked your cows, shoveled manure, pulled weeds and delivered flowers and vegetables. And you slaughtered chickens, paid the feed bill and schooled and fed the kids, then jumped in to read my book, give me feedback and cheer me on, and support me through all the highs and lows that come with farming and writing a book at the same time.

Farmers are the best people I have ever met, and each one of you in our book launch group is an extraordinary being and have chosen one of the most honorable vocations. I consider each of you a friend. It's been a joy to meet several of you in person in your travels or mine. Thank you for being here and for being a part of this book.